THE W

Tom Kelly

Acknowledgements

Some of these poems appeared in the following publications: *John Donne in Jarrow* (Here Now, 1993), *Their Lives* (Tears in the Fence, 1995), *That Time of life* (KT Publications, 2002), *The Picture From Here* (Sand Publications, 2004).

Thanks are due to the editors of the following magazines where some of these poems were first published : 3x4, *Coffee House Poetry, Doors, The Frogmore Papers, Hybrid, Iota, Iron, Obsessed by Pipework, Odyssey, Other Poetry, Penniless Press, Purple Patch, The Red Lamp, The Rialto, Slipstream, The Third Half, The Ugly Tree, The Yellow Crane.*

Thanks also to The Customs House, South Shields, whose Arts Development programme enabled Tom Kelly to write the sequence devoted to the paintings of Norman Cornish.

Published 2007
by

Smokestack Books
PO Box 408, Middlesbrough TS5 6WA
e-mail : info@smokestack-books.co.uk
www.smokestack-books.co.uk

Cover design by James Cianciaruso

Printed by
EPW Print & Design Ltd

ISBN 0-9551061-7-6
ISBN 978-0-955-10617-0

Author's photograph: Craig Leng ©

Two Men at Bar with Dog by Norman Cornish (c)
Northumbria University Permanent Collection.

Smokestack Books
gratefully acknowledges the support of
Middlesbrough Borough Council
and Arts Council North East

Smokestack Books is a member of
Independent Northern Publishers
www.northernpublishers.co.uk
and is represented by Inpress Ltd
www.inpressbooks.co.uk

Contents

the wrong jarrow

For Andy Willoughby

In the wrong Jarrow
there's no cobbled streets
no men hunched round corners
eyeing up the ground
there's no gas lamps and hobnailed boots
singing down Ellison Street
there's no one gathering around the Town Hall with banners
and the Bishop Of Durham
isn't saying it's wrong.

It's the wrong Jarrow
the hunger should be more real
like in some African state
trousers should be shiny, threadbare
there should be more hate
policemen should use truncheons more
let's see more blood
broken bones.

This is the wrong Jarrow
poverty needs to be more visible
this is the wrong Jarrow
there's unemployment and deprivation
and no steel works and shipyard and the club's are dead
and there's problem estates and no go areas
and drugs on tap.
But it's the wrong Jarrow
it's not what I want
not what I want at all.
I'll come back when it's burning.

jarrow slag heap, 1933

from a photograph

Palmer's shipyard closed.
Three years to the Crusade.
Six years to war.

Working on the Slag Heap,
Palmer's off-white
waste mountain
running through it
dark as blood.

Digging, shovelling.
Hard work.
Low pay.

Poor men working on slag.

the blood pit, jarrow

I've got this photograph Blu-tacked on my wall,
five men staring at the camera,
knowing precisely who they are.

It's late in the 1930s; they are at the Blood Pit,
two or three of them are boxers
they've got that look:
hit me, I'll smash you back.

There's one in the middle
that smiles, he must be a manager
of sorts, he has his arms round the others.

No sign of any blood.

my kind of town i

Bread and lard tastes
so good, fills the belly,
fights cold
that sucks everything,
your desire
to go on, inch on, march on
giving way to anger that pisses like bile, scalds.

There is no way out,
escape impossible,
peel and
strip more pain
- dried skin that's torn into shreds.

At the corner
they kill time
as time kills them.
Nowt.
'Nowt' stamped on foreheads
leaden hands and hearts.

He's working in the timber yard.
Not living at home.
Surviving that's all and bitterness
a ball stuck in his throat
and no matter how much he coughs
it's still there even as I watched his eyes grey,
mist like mercury he could have ladled out.

my kind of town ii

Did he dream of creeping into their warm homes,
the house settling into comfortable sleep
warmth drifting into the loft where a rocking horse eyes him
raise their bedclothes and lift pillows
see them struggle to death. Someone must pay
he snarls at the gaping wound of hunger that eats him
everyday and night and he prays that dreams
will spread solace through just one day. One day. Please.
Not a lot to ask.

Granny is hit again. Tears prickle
down her cheeks. I feel my legs
and rub away her pain but I can't. Of course I can't.
The stick comes down again.
Men did that then: raise you hand, lift your fist
and bury it in your face. Feel her hurt.

And there's blood on the streets
the polis is dragging Wilfie Page,
the crowd are shouting
and me dad's there.

My town's got blood on the streets,
they're reading the Riot Act
and hunger's a badge posted
on every stomach.

There's blood on the cobbles
as he's dragged by his feet to the cells,
blood on the streets
in my town.

1964

There's frost on the inside of the windows,
cold freezes my nose, makes me cling to the blankets,
wrap my feet into a ball, lie still.
I switch on the light,
it doesn't have a shade,
and it screws my eyes like a used lemon.

Walking to work I cut into the frost,
join the procession, heads bowed.

I make lists of what I'll buy,
strips of paper in my pocket, stiff with dreams.

It's the back end of 1964
and my arse doesn't hang out of my trousers,
and having the right shoes, jacket, shirt,
rises above everything
that life can throw at me.

after the bleep

My dad's left a message
on our answer machine
and I can't make out,
with his usual stuttering,
it's something about me but I'd be guessing
and then I wake
remembering he's been dead
over nine years
and we don't have an answer machine.

message on a bottle

Seaham Colliery explosion 1880

Singing hymns with his son
in that sad enclave,
scratching love-lines on a tin water bottle
'Learn the children to pray for me',
death inevitable as the failing light
that smudged forty men and boys.

Today I told my daughter
that this stone was coal,
that it gave warmth,
burning like a prayer
in the cold dark.

more

I should have done more,
taken you to the park
climbed up the steps
chased round the ten bob bit
until I was sick as you shouted more
- I just should have done more.

Now she's on the telephone
to her friends more
and she talks about her hair more
and she doesn't want to run to the park
walk down our 'secret path'
that's now made of tarmac
and the branches don't attack you
and we don't scurry down the mud
to the park where tiddlers dart in shoals
and you don't talk about that any more.

bewick woodcut

He's almost lost among trees,
belly pressed against a branch;
the branch cutting his skin.
In negative, the line cuts the river
waiting for a bite, a wet line,
taut, wriggling with life.
The water's above his ankles,
aching with cold
but the bite
has him forgetting.
A church in the distance,
a spire, eavesdrops,
holds everything.

believe

It's happening, the odd crocus
edges out between rocks and trees,
blue tongues licking crisp sunshine
at the feet of near-stripped trees;
telling us it's becoming warmer and lighter,
forcing us to believe
that there's life after hard-bitten hail,
snow and frost that sprayed our breath
in those black mornings.

the river again

The river's mute, an ex-caulker-burner
knows he's a dinosaur
walking his security guard beat
when a shovel of memories
hits him hard, has him floored
rekindling flames
of his trade he knows is extinct.

A voice on a tape, an out-take from history
struck me like a wet clout,
shocking me into the past,
my struggling voice remembered
in the nooks and crannies
that make up your past:
shipyard, river bank, back streets
beat and heart beat of a thousand workers
slamming streets
where women clasp corners
waiting for their men
feeling like catchers
grabbing white hot rivets of money
before their men spend wages on anything
but on what they should.

art form

He stands at the window
examines the road,
checking for imperfections
on the surface
of anything.

He's plausible
reasonable
nothing's ever his fault.

He'll tell you anything
you don't want to hear,
the rest he clouds
in vagueness he's got off
to an art-form.

afternoon session

He wakes at six o'clock,
head aching, tongue furred, blowing his nose
in the toilet, pissing in the centre of the bowl,
checking his pocket for change,
the price of two or three pints.

The session started at eleven,
the bar had just opened,
smelling of Jeyes fluid and fag ends.
He drank four pints before twelve.
By one he was well gone.
Somebody sang Danny Boy at two.
At three there was a fight.
He left at four.

the estate

'No' is the password, stamped on their hopes.
It's cheap, quick, used like a gun,
bitter as vinegar.
Christ-like they're fed sponges,
sopping with bile.

Some of them share
most don't.

Water's on the meter.
Debt is automatic.
Tattoos serve as a warning,
badges of an army.

The estate has boundaries,
leaders and also rans
sharing losing like scars.

The police helicopter's
a gigantic moth
circling grubby lives.

waiting

for Swan Hunters, Hawthorne Leslies, Palmers

The bus stop has fewer passengers waiting
at seven o'clock in the morning.

More women now,
they huddle and flick cigarettes
that pin prick the gloom,
odd laughs hitting the silence.

The yards are finished.
Kids need to be told where the river is
and the cranes aren't a fairground.

Some still believe
the river will return:
tankers and refits, the lot!

Delusions,
and fewer passengers are waiting.

and now that

And now that
he can watch the clock for hours
and now that
he can count the bricks on the far wall
and now that
he knows next door's every record
and now that
he's joined the gang of statistics
and now that
he can't adjust his hands and fingers
and now that
time is an obese burden
and now that
he knows it's always going to be this way
he handles it badly.

another time, another place

He fancied a walk:
park awash
with drifting kids
and dogs.

He didn't notice:
houses demolished
the steel works rubble,
river and steel blue sky.

He didn't notice himself:
battered brown mac,
black slip-ons, slipping off his feet,
grey trousers creased
above his ankles.

Under his dead eyes,
and soft hands shoved in his pockets,
he had a picture
different from this.

john donne in jarrow

Not that long ago,
on my way to the pub,
I saw a man standing at his back door
looking at the sky,
examining early evening light,
flying past
into his dark kitchen.
I imagined thick grease around a cooker,
windows closed tight
but for that moment
he appeared in a great world of air and angels.

taxi

And what happens when the redundancy money runs out
and you just have to snap your eyes
and there's a taxi at you
and all factories and offices are padlocked
and schools and colleges are landscaped
and it's all a surprise I suppose
and what happens when we all pass our driving tests
and no-one wants a lift
and the work on the rigs is drying-up
and reality's been relocated
and kids can't spell prospects
and reports bleed lies
and everyone in the know conspires
and what happens when everyone's a taxi driver.

days

Steer clear of the street,
no make that the entire town,
it'll drag you down
have you wishing
for anything but here,
the place you visit
but don't live in now.

'I only go for funerals',
seeing the hearse
moaning up the cemetery bank,
in the lowest gear
in the hardest of days.

street

It's cold tonight,
there's a sliver of frost
on top of the car.
My child can't sleep
she coughs
above the whispering television,
abandons her dreams
in tatters,
a shredded plastic bag
in a bare March tree.

Tomorrow will be better.

empty glass

It's a slow death,
taking a day at a time
and filling it
with what will eventually kill him.

The stomach swells,
lies over his taut belt,
sagging, juggling along.

The face shows strain,
blood vessels sit on the surface,
turn more and more vivid,
I'm sure he glows in the dark.

Legs become unreliable,
won't do as they should
and it's another hospital visit
after he head butts
the snooker table.

Now his mouth searches for words,
eyes glisten
and his glass is empty.

their river

A female Fagin selling drugs,
drinking, flirting and nodding sagely
to boys that could be her sons,
watching their eyes droop,
heavy as broken doors, smashed windows...

One of this merry band
lifts a pint, taking minutes to reach his lips,
then steadily, carefully, returning it
to the beer mat,
he smiles with satisfaction:
a job well done.

The old men watch, they have worked
in factories, on the river, built heavy machines,
broken nails and fingers,
shake their heads at young men sold
up and down their river.

one day

He's built it up
beer belly,
hard look, same as his mates.

She's got it:
tight short skirt,
loads of make-up,
chewing, smoking and talking at the same time.

They've got a place together,
two kids,
one to another lad.

He carries the bairn on his shoulders,
'One day this will be yours'
tattooed in the sky.

game

The moment before waking
when you can remake everything,
turn clocks back and forward
at will, any time you want
and you play that dark early morning game
to your hearts content or raw and you are woken
by the alarm and painful memories
that will not budge
and they are not prepared
to give in
to your demands

getting by badly

It's trying not to think about the aggravation
& damp shoes and that bar of stress across my back,
& it's the waking up two hours before you have to
& re-runs of crap days and what I should have said
& it's all the things you know & don't know
& it's coming back at you, fresh and bright as new paint
& we could do without it: definitely, quite easily,
just ignore this business of getting by badly.

all that's left

I'm listening to simmering rain,
& remembering more than I want.
This is a holding your breath moment, like a pause,
life suspended;
answers searched for, left unopened on the carpet
like the results of tests or a winner, another Dead Cert
heading for the Knacker's Yard.
en route to what we'd rather avoid
and now it's too late,
what we have is me & you: this is the moment
saying what we feel is all that's left.

nostalgia kid

Twenty years ago it was milk & honey,
Garden of Eden had nothing on those days.
Beer two pence a pint, everybody smiled,
you know I'm right, kids were great. Not like now.
I was never ill, didn't feel the cold and
I couldn't stop smiling and you know it's true.
You knew me, what I was like, the life and soul
of all night parties, money not a problem.
Friends would ring day and night: the clubs were jumping.
Best years of me life: Nothing like now. Shit days.
Everything's dead, like a bloody cemetery.
You could live, not like now: go on buy me a pint.

shadows

See them
tripping out the pub
ready for a fight,
belligerence an art form:
the snarl, half closed eyes,
spitting too near
and then they disappear
pissing off down an alley
lost in shadows
that turn up
in your dreams.

a problem shared

And the best way to confront something
is to firmly turn your back on it,
that's the way.
Don't think about the problem
because it'll go away, I promise.
Some sudden breeze will pick it up
and it'll be gone, like magic.
Rely on me. Do the same as me,
we'll bury our heads together: you go first,
dig a hole approximately 12 inches in diameter,
place your head in, I'll do the same.

elegy

The yard's
dead, quiet

chains no longer
hold onto ships
onto lives.

**Poems inspired by
the paintings and drawings of Spennymoor
artist, Norman Cornish**

colliery road and man

He's got nowt to tell,
nowt you'd want to hear.

There is light, salvation,
singing in bars and
laughter at home and
all that carry-on
but tonight there's drizzle
that dewdrops from his nose
and an ache that burns.

The fence is half cut,
hitting the field, lying on its back,
it's always like this,

he knows every step
of his road
and it gets no easier.

the faces are ours

I've just found me Granda, Tot, never knew he smoked cigarettes,
it was always a pipe that he smacked and then spat on the fire.
There he is, there, among all those faces, laughing
well, not quite. Never was much of a laugher. The faces
are ours, uncle Billy that was terrified
of buying a round and uncle Tommy that would give you his last
if he had it that day. Then there's Jackie, dyed-in-the
wool Communist,
no hymns at his funeral; always dapper, articulate and sad.

still a lad

Coal dust bags his lungs, he loses phlegm
on the way to the pub. Smoke mists his face,
waters his eyes; his cap's stuck at a jaunty angle,
under all of this he's still a lad.

man alone

I'm drawn to him, something about his nose,
the way he holds his hands, remembering a caress years away.
His eyes are masked but you know they are not with you.

The bar's busy
but he's alone. No smile for the camera,
disappointment anoints him,
might-have-beens tear him to shreds.

He is outside every company, 'He's best ignored',
somebody once said. He wears a muffler
and his shirt's worn out. His ex-working hands
soft as a bairns as he searches for a callous
to recall who he was. All he finds is an old man's hands.

men at the bar

Shoulders nudging,
whispers and guffaws,

might as well have a bit crack.
The cemetery's dead quiet.

misty day

      Looking up Edward Street
mist holds St Paul's Church,
traps that crown at the top of the street.
A woman pushes a pram and drags an older child
who wants to be anywhere but there. All the windows are
grey, no colour
to redress the scene.

      You hear notes of near silence,
the woman's receding stilettos, the child's cry,
you feel the church will go, a conjurers sleight of hand,
there would just be a gap, a new vista, the mist extended
with no one answering.

      This is the moment before it goes,
the time you will remember before the history bailiffs
do a reconstruction brick by brick,
rebuild a world, make memory of this.

fish and chip shop

Two bairns face the street,
money sweats in the palm of their hands, they say
over and over, 'four chips, two fish, plenty of batter.'

Rain's hitting home and they head there;
a woman pushes a pram as her husband shuffles in her footsteps,
dogs decide whether to square up to one another,
woman triangle the corner and
I can taste fish and chips and me glasses mist over,
there's fairy washing on the road
and the first house of the pictures starts in half an hour
and it's time I was home and it's time and another fish
sprinkles in the fryer and I head home with me fish and chips
keeping me warm as I'll ever feel.

two women

Two large sherries for the big ladies in their seats.
They know everyone, by their coughs and walks and
everyone knows them. Conversation's a leaky tap, and
a nod, wink, twist of a mouth is all that's needed.

By themselves now, they make do with each other.

A son comes in on a Thursday night, sends over a drink,
they return weak smiles.

Three drinks before the shuffle from behind their table.
They go their separate ways at the corner,
the sherry a chalice,
warming them, lulling them into drowsy sleep.

'See ya tomorrow.' 'If ah'm spared,' they don't say.

telegraph poles

I'd pray if I wasn't so tired and lie down here and sleep
in these fields if I could. Me hands are tender, my fingers won't
unite in prayer.
I'm not old.
Hunger's clawing at me. The street's moving away
like a dream. Christ's mad on the cross and he hasn't had a shift
and I'm full as hell. That's where I'll end up thinking like that.
Pray for me dear wife. God aa'm clammin'.

newcastle supporter

Me lad bought the season ticket. Aa've seen all th'greats,
Milburn...now aa sit beside a solicitor.
Mind, aa won't wear aa shirt, the grandson does
he lives down south, when he's up here we go together
- aa've got to speak slowly to him.

Th' world's changed
aa haven't. It's different and aa'm not crying,
not that you'd ever see me tears.

three men

Three bandy-legged men,
haversacks propped
on aching backs
nod their heads home
close as sin,
telling their tale, reliving the shift
before they go.

They live as close as can be,
fighting elements
living on the brink
that can blast them away,
they know only the moment counts.